Rajiv Sharma is a Public Law Barrister and member of the Public Law and Human Rights team at The 36 Group Chambers. He has appeared in many important cases at all levels of the Court system from the Tribunals to the Senior Courts. Rajiv has appeared before the Courts as leading Counsel and his area of speciality is Immigration Law.

Rajiv is a fierce advocate and does not shy away from making difficult or aggressive arguments, where necessary.

Rajiv is also engaged in advising the next generation of practitioners and takes pride in his role as a Visiting Lecturer, particularly the work involving teaching on the professional courses.

A Practical Guide to Long Residence Applications Under the Immigration Rules

A Practical Guide to Long Residence Applications Under the Immigration Rules

Rajiv Sharma

Barrister

Law Brief Publishing

Published 2022 by Law Brief Publishing, an imprint of Law Brief Publishing Ltd
30 The Parks
Minehead
Somerset
TA24 8BT

www.lawbriefpublishing.com

Paperback: 978-1-914608-47-6

ਮਾਂ ਦੀ ਪੂਜਾ ਰੱਬ ਦੀ ਪੂਜਾ
ਮਾਂ ਰੱਬ ਦਾ ਰੂਪ ਹੈ ਦੂਜਾ

For my parents, my brothers,
China, Maahi, Rajvir and Viyaan.

PREFACE

'This Court has very frequently in recent years had to deal with appeals arising out of difficulties in understanding the Immigration Rules. This is partly a result of their labyrinthine structure and idiosyncratic drafting conventions but sometimes it is a simple matter of the confused language and/or structure of particular provisions. This case is a particularly egregious example.'

Underhill LJ in *Hoque & Ors v The Secretary of State for the Home Department* [2020] EWCA Civ 1357 addressing the drafting of the Rules with which this book is concerned.

At first glance the Long Residence provisions of the **Immigration Rules** may seem straightforward. Unfortunately, as with many other provisions of the rules, it has been shown through successive litigation in the Higher Courts that this is not the case.

Issues have arisen over two linked requirements, in particular; (i) the continuity of the residence; and (ii) the lawfulness of the residence.

This book will look to focus on difficulties arising out of those two issues, aiming to provide possible solutions in advance whilst also considering the other requirements within the rules.

The law stated in this book is believed to be correct as of 01-11-2022.

Special thanks to Dr Estévez de la Rosa and his team at Hospiten Sur who allowed me a week of peace and quiet to get this book written.

Rajiv Sharma
November 2022

CONTENTS

Chapter One   Introduction   1

Chapter Two   What Do We Mean by   3
'Long Residence'?

Chapter Three   The Requirements Broadly   11

Chapter Four   Statutory Extension   15

Chapter Five   10 Years' Residence Accrued   21
During Statutory Extension

Chapter Six   Applications by Overstayers   29

Chapter Seven   Other Decisions of the Courts   43

Chapter Eight   Breaks in Continuity   53

Chapter Nine   Discretion   61

Chapter Ten   Other Considerations   71

Chapter Eleven   Conclusions   75

CHAPTER ONE

INTRODUCTION

Immigration is a fact of life. There are a variety of reasons why one may wish to relocate including to seek safety, to seek further education, for work or for family etc.

A natural consequence of relocation is the upheaval of an established life and the establishment of new roots. It follows therefore that the longer an individual remains in one place the deeper their roots in that place will have settled.

This natural consequence is recognised within the Immigration Rules which set two alternate criteria for those wishing to settle on the basis of roots not set out in other categories (i.e. those who cannot apply on the basis of family life, for example).

Those two criteria are:

(1) To establish a right to remain based (broadly) on 10 years' lawful residence; or

(2) To establish 20 years' continuous residence (whether lawfully or otherwise).

Both categories could linguistically be called 'long residence' categories but only one comes under that technical heading.

In the following chapter we discuss what practitioners mean when referring to 'long residence'

CHAPTER TWO

WHAT DO WE MEAN
BY 'LONG RESIDENCE'?

Long residence under the Immigration Rules has a specific meaning. Until the 9th of July 2012 the Immigration Rules contained two routes under the 'Long Residence' Provisions; one covering continuous lawful residence i.e. where an applicant had some form of visa or permission to be in the United Kingdom throughout the period; and another covering other periods i.e. where an applicant had some form of visa or permission to be in the United Kingdom for only some or even none of the period.

There were thus two routes and they were referred to as the 'lawful residence' and 'unlawful residence' provisions within the Long Residence Rules.

In June 2012 as part of a wider shake-up of the Immigration Rules (seen by some as the start of the 'hostile environment)[1], the decision was announced to remove or delete the 'unlawful residence' part of the Long Residence Rules[2].

Included in that announcement was the introduction of a new 'Private Life' route to be found under **paragraph 276ADE(1)**. That route included a provision for 'unlawful residence' of adults but increased the period of residence required from 14 years (under the pre-July

---

[1] The Hostile Environment explained | Joint Council for the Welfare of Immigrants (jcwi.org.uk)

[2] Statement of changes in immigration rules HC 194 (publishing.service.gov.uk)

2012 rules) to 20 years as well as increasing the length of time an applicant under that route would need to wait to be able to permanently settle in the United Kingdom.

The entire 'Private Life' route has been moved again and can now be found under **Appendix Private Life** with the specific 20-year residence requirement being found at **PL 5.1(a)**. The move was brought about by a statement of changes (statement to parliament by which the Rules themselves can be changed) laid before parliament on the 15th of March 2022[3]. The explanatory memorandum[4] (the document prepared by the Home Office to explain the purpose and aim of the changes) says the following about the nature of the change:

> 'Introduction of the new Appendix Settlement Family Life and new Appendix Private Life
>
> 7.27 Appendix Settlement Family Life and Appendix Private Life replace existing provisions. Changes are being made to how these routes deal with validity of applications. The requirements currently set out in paragraph 34 of the Immigration Rules will now be in part replaced by validity rules in Appendix Private Life and Appendix Settlement Family Life which state:
>
> - The application must be made on the specified form on GOV.UK;
>
> - Any fee and Immigration Health Charge must have been paid;

---

[3] Statement of Changes in Immigration Rules – HC 1118 (publishing.service.gov.uk)

[4] Explanatory Memorandum to HC 1118 (publishing.service.gov.uk)

- The applicant must have provided any required biometrics;

- The applicant must have provided a passport or other document which satisfactorily establishes their identity and nationality; and

- A person applying for settlement must meet specified rules as to the current or previous permission held.

7.28 These validity rules do not represent significant policy change. Validity requirements for dependants are being aligned with other routes (see administrative changes in paragraph 7.43 and 7.44). Minor and technical changes are being made to ensure cross references are consistent with the new appendices.

7.29 Changes are being introduced which affect applications for settlement under Appendix Private Life and Appendix Settlement Family Life:

- Applicants will be able to combine time on family and private life routes towards the qualifying period rather than having to 'reset the clock' on the qualifying period if their circumstances change, though they will need to complete at least a year in their current route;

- Applicants will be able to count time on other routes to settlement where certain conditions are met;

- Individuals who have a criminal conviction leading to a custodial sentence of 12 months or more will not be able to qualify for settlement;

- Individuals who have a criminal conviction leading to a custodial sentence of less than 12 months will not be able to qualify for settlement unless the applicant has completed a qualifying period of 10 years and has completed 5 compliant years with permission on family and private life routes since the end of that sentence;

- Applicants who take part in a sham marriage / civil partnership, use false documents or provide false information in an immigration application, use deception, owe unpaid litigation debt to the Home Office or unpaid debt over £500 to the NHS, or who breach immigration conditions during their qualifying period will ned to complete 10 years qualifying period, including 5 years continuous residence with permission since this came to the attention of the Home Office, before they qualify for settlement. Applicants who enter the UK illegally (except for children and young adults between the ages of 18-25 on the private life route) will need to complete a 10-year qualifying period before settlement;

- Applicants for settlement will be able to rely on GCSE, A Levels or equivalent Scottish Higher qualifications in English language or literature following education in a UK school to show they meet the English language requirement (these changes are reflected in Appendix English language).'

Given the effective severing of the 'unlawful residence' route from the 'lawful residence' route the former is no longer considered a 'Long Residence' route even if that is what is logically catered for. Because it does not form part of the scope of 'long residence' given its legal definition, it also falls outside of the scope of this book.

This book will therefore focus on the remaining, 'lawful residence' route. This route has been subject to incremental change over time[5] and most recently some 'violence' has been done to the drafting of the provision (i.e. how it is written and read) by the Courts in order for the provisions to make more sense. This will be explored further with reference to the Judicial comments in the relevant cases.

As we have seen in the preface, the government has been called out for the complexity of the rules in this and other areas before. So far most attempts to simplify the rules in a piecemeal fashion (usually by the creation of specific Appendices to the Immigration Rules) have not been enough and the Courts have commented that the entire system is unfit for purpose rather suggesting a more radical wholesale change may be more appropriate[6].

Jackson LJ was so concerned with the state of the Rules that he stated the following in his Judgment in *Pokhriyal v Secretary of State for the Home Department* [2013] EWCA Civ 1568

> '[4] … These provisions have now achieved a degree of complexity which even the Byzantine Emperors would have envied.'

Indeed the Law Commission, an independent body tasked with reviewing existing law and recommending reform where necessary, describes the make-up of the Rules as follows:

> 'Their structure is confusing and numbering inconsistent. Provisions overlap with identical or near identical wording.

---

[5] A consideration of drafting changes is set out in the Judgment in *Hoque* from [72] – [83]

[6] See, for example, *Alvi, R (on the application of) v Secretary of State for the Home Department* [2012] UKSC 33

> The drafting style, often including multiple cross-references, can be impenetrable. The frequency of change fuels complexity.'[7]

The primary recommendation within the report (with unanimous support from all consultees) was 'that the Immigration Rules be overhauled.'[8]

This idea is not new, with previous Home Secretary The Right Honourable John Reid MP[9] referring to the Home Office's immigration operation as "not fit for purpose"[10].

In relation to the rules for Long Residence, there have been governmental assurances that the rules will be re-drafted (rewritten), see below, but at the time of writing this book that is yet to happen.

At the time of writing (October 2022) we in the last week of a (catastrophic) Liz Truss premiership[11] and Suella Braverman (ex-junior-junior Treasury Counsel – Barrister instructed on behalf of the government) was Home Secretary until she was replaced by Grant Shapps, after having to step down for breaching the ministerial code, become the shortest serving Home Secretary (so far). It remains to be seen what changes, if any, are made under the next incarnation of the Tory government.

---

[7] Simplification of the Immigration Rules (2019) Law Commission Consultation Paper No 242, paras 1.4 to 1.6.

[8] Law Commission Simplification of the Immigration Rules: Report

[9] Now Lord Reid of Cardowan

[10] BBC NEWS | Politics | Immigration system unfit – Reid

[11] She has announced her resignation but not yet stepped down.

Until those changes are made, the rules explored in this book are likely to continue to govern long residence applications.

CHAPTER THREE

THE REQUIREMENTS BROADLY

The requirements of the Rules can be found at <u>Immigration Rules – Immigration Rules part 7: other categories – Guidance – GOV.UK (www.gov.uk)</u> and so will not be copied in full. The most relevant parts are copied below but reference should be made to the entirety when making any application:

'276B. The requirements to be met by an applicant for indefinite leave to remain on the ground of long residence in the United Kingdom are that:

(i) (a) he has had at least 10 years continuous lawful residence in the United Kingdom.

(ii) having regard to the public interest there are no reasons why it would be undesirable for him to be given indefinite leave to remain on the ground of long residence, taking into account his:

(a) age; and

(b) strength of connections in the United Kingdom; and

(c) personal history, including character, conduct, associations and employment record; and

(d) domestic circumstances; and

(e) compassionate circumstances; and

(f) any representations received on the person's behalf; and

(iii) the applicant does not fall for refusal under the general grounds for refusal.

(iv) the applicant has demonstrated sufficient knowledge of the English language and sufficient knowledge about life in the United Kingdom, in accordance with Appendix KoLL.

(v) the applicant must not be in the UK in breach of immigration laws, except that, where paragraph 39E of these Rules applies, any current period of overstaying will be disregarded. Any previous period of overstaying between periods of leave will also be disregarded where –

(a) the previous application was made before 24 November 2016 and within 28 days of the expiry of leave; or

(b) the further application was made on or after 24 November 2016 and paragraph 39E of these Rules applied.'

In subsequent chapters we will look at the manner in which the Court of Appeal has reformulated the above in order to be able to sensibly interpret the rules. The rule set out above is how it appears on the gov.uk website i.e. in its proper form prior to reformulation by the Court of Appeal. We will see the reformulation below in chapter six.

Broadly speaking, the requirements can be summarised as below:

(a) Continuous residence of at least 10 years;

(b) Lawfulness of residence for at least 10-continuous years;

(c) Taking into account the personal circumstances, there is no reason not to grant such leave;

(d) The Applicant does not fall foul of any general grounds for refusal;

(e) Appendix KOLL is satisfied; and

(f) The Applicant must not be in breach of any Immigration Rules.

As discussed in the introduction above, each of these requirements, on the face of it, should be fairly uncomplicated to resolve. But perhaps because of their interaction with one another (for example requirements (a) and (b) or (b) and (f) as summarised above) how they are to be interpreted is far more complex than would have originally seemed the case.

In the following chapters we will consider some of those complexities.

CHAPTER FOUR

STATUTORY EXTENSION

As can be seen from the Rules set out in the preceding chapter, when an applicant has actually[12] had leave to remain throughout the relevant ten-year period they should be in a position to satisfy 276B(i)(a) – *the ten-year requirement.*

In the proceeding chapters we will address the situation that arises when, during the relevant ten-year period, leave to remain expires. Those chapters will look at where continuity is broken or where the continuity of legality is broken.

In the instant chapter we will address the discreet issue of the situation in which leave to remain would have expired but has not – *the statutory extension.*

A grant of limited leave to remain is accompanied by a notice which contains, among other things, information on when that limited leave will expire. If the recipient does nothing at the end of that period their leave to remain will end – they will be overstayers for the purposes of the Immigration Rules[13].

---

[12] As opposed to that leave to remain having expired or when that leave to remain is deemed to have expired.

[13] There are or were certain exemptions. For example, pre-withdrawal from the EU, those who became family members of EEA Citizens did not need to apply prior to expiry of leave to reman, but their entitlement to remain fell in legal provisions outside of the Immigration Rules and so they would have been technical overstayers but exempt through policy (and international law) from treatment as such.

However, those that validly applied in-time for an extension or variation of that leave to remain were protected by a statutory extension of their leave to remain if an application was undecided prior to the date on which leave would have expired. This automatic statutory extension was pursuant to s3C of the **Immigration Act 1971**.

'3C Continuation of leave pending variation decision

(1)   This section applies if—

(a) a person who has limited leave to enter or remain in the United Kingdom applies to the Secretary of State for variation of the leave,

(b) the application for variation is made before the leave expires, and

(c) the leave expires without the application for variation having been decided.

(2)   The leave is extended by virtue of this section during any period when—

(a) the application for variation is neither decided nor withdrawn,

(b) an appeal under section 82(1) of the Nationality, Asylum and Immigration Act 2002 could be brought [, while the appellant is in the United Kingdom]2 against the decision on the application for variation (ignoring any possibility of an appeal out of time with permission),

(c) an appeal under that section against that decision [, brought while the appellant is in the United Kingdom,]4 is pending (within the meaning of section 104 of that Act) [, [...]6]5

(ca) an appeal could be brought under the Immigration (Citizens' Rights Appeals) (EU Exit) Regulations 2020 ("the 2020 Regulations"), while the appellant is in the United Kingdom, against the decision on the application for variation (ignoring any possibility of an appeal out of time with permission),

(cb) an appeal under the 2020 Regulations against that decision, brought while the appellant is in the United Kingdom, is pending (within the meaning of those Regulations), or

(d) an administrative review of the decision on the application for variation—

(i) could be sought, or

(ii) is pending.

(3) Leave extended by virtue of this section shall lapse if the applicant leaves the United Kingdom.

(3A) Leave extended by virtue of this section may be cancelled if the applicant—

(a) has failed to comply with a condition attached to the leave, or

(b) has used or uses deception in seeking leave to remain (whether successfully or not).

(4)   A person may not make an application for variation of his leave to enter or remain in the United Kingdom while that leave is extended by virtue of this section.

(5)   But subsection (4) does not prevent the variation of the application mentioned in subsection (1)(a).

(6)   The Secretary of State may make regulations determining when an application is decided for the purposes of this section; and the regulations–

   (a) may make provision by reference to receipt of a notice,

   (b) may provide for a notice to be treated as having been received in specified circumstances,

   (c) may make different provision for different purposes or circumstances,

   (d) shall be made by statutory instrument, and

   (e) shall be subject to annulment in pursuance of a resolution of either House of Parliament.

(7)   In this section— *"administrative review"* means a review conducted under the immigration rules; the question of whether an administrative review is pending is to be determined in accordance with the immigration rules.'

We see, therefore, that this provision provides for an extension of leave to remain in circumstances in which an applicant makes an application prior to expiry of leave (considered by the Court of Appeal to be an 'in time' application[14]) and that application is undecided by the time leave to remain would have expired.

We see from the decision in *MU ('statement of additional grounds'; long residence; discretion) Bangladesh* [2010] UKUT 442 (IAC) that the senior presenting officer for the Secretary of State accepted in that case that leave to remain was '[6] lawful for the purposes of paragraph 276B(i)(a), in that it was "*pursuant to existing leave to enter or remain*" as specified by paragraph 276A(b)(i) ... includ[ing] the 'statutorily extended leave' under section 3C of the 1971 Act'.

The statutory extension continues whilst any appeal lodged in-time remains undecided. This includes any further in-time appeals to the Upper Tribunal, as shown by the facts in the case of *MU Bangladesh* itself, or even to the Court of Appeal on statutory appeal and beyond. This will not include any challenges to the refusal of permission to appeal against a decision of the First-tier Tribunal by the Upper Tribunal – such challenges would by way of Judicial Review and therefore are not Statutory challenges and fall out-with the statutory extension. The situation that arises from success in such challenges will be addressed below.

---

[14] See *Secretary of State for the Home Department v Ali* [2021] EWCA Civ 1357

CHAPTER FIVE

10 YEARS' RESIDENCE ACCRUED DURING STATUTORY EXTENSION

Having established that an individual may be able to accrue the ten years' residence required to apply for indefinite leave to remain under this route whilst an application or appeal are left pending the next question is what an applicant should do if they find themselves in such a position.

The answer to that question will depend upon the circumstances and indeed there may also be an alternative to any action being required at all, is some scenarios.

The headings below reflect broadly applicable circumstances in which an applicant may find themselves:

In-time application is undecided

If an in-time application has been made and the applicant has accrued the necessary residence period whilst the application is undecided the applicant is entitled to vary that application to seek consideration under the long residence route for settlement.

The ability to vary a pending application was established in *JH (Zimbabwe) v Secretary of State for the Home Department* [2009] EWCA Civ 78, in which Richards LJ confirms the following:

'[40] … a later application is capable of being treated as a variation of the first application even if it is for a different purpose and on a different form.'

This was subsequently helpfully summarised in *Hoque & Ors v The Secretary of State for the Home Department* [2020] EWCA Civ 1357, in which the facts are relevant to the current topic (i.e. the (purported) accrual of ten years' continuous lawful residence), as follows:

'[16] where an applicant for leave to remain on one basis is pending it is open to him or her to make a further application on a different basis, which is treated as a variation of the original application: see *JH (Zimbabwe) v Secretary of State for the Home Department* [2009] EWCA Civ 78'

Per Underhill LJ

Indeed this position is reflected within The Home Office casework instructions which state that *'[A]n applicant can vary the purpose of an application at any time before a decision on the application is served. Any application submitted where a previous application has not yet been decided is a variation of that previous application. An applicant can only have one application outstanding at any one time'*.[15]

The variation will need to be compliant with **paragraph 34** of the Immigration Rules including the use of a specified form and payment of the necessary fee (currently £2,404 for settlement) and, of course, the provision of the relevant evidence including the evidence to satisfy the KOLL requirements.

---

[15] Validation, variation and withdrawal of applications.docx (publishing.service.gov.uk)

This should allow the decision-maker to consider the application under the long residence route for settlement thus allowing the original applicant to be granted indefinite leave to remain (subject to satisfying the requirements within **paragraph 276B**) and, crucially, will be considered a Human Rights application such that any refusal will carry a right of appeal for the purposes of **s 82** of the **Nationality, Immigration and Asylum Act 2002** (the 2002 Act), subject to certification under **section 94**.

The last element (acceptance of the claim as a human rights claim) is important for three reasons:

(1) Firstly, because having accepted that the claim is a human rights claim entitles an applicant faced with a refusal to challenge that refusal before an independent Judge of the First Tier Tribunal (Immigration and Asylum Chamber) (FtT). This acceptance is particularly important where the original application (i.e. the one being varied) would not have given rise to a statutory right of appeal[16].;

(2) Secondly, these Judges are equipped to consider the facts of the case and reach a decision independent of that taken by the decision-maker. Although their remit is limited by **s 84** of the **2002 Act** namely that the grounds of appeal are limited to protection or human rights grounds it is by now trite that the ability to satisfy the rules (particularly those that fall within the Human Rights grounds i.e. private life, family life etc) is

---

[16] For example, many individuals seeking indefinite leave to remain on the basis of routes under the Points Based System are unable to challenge refusals solely under that route.

sufficient for an FtT Judge to allow an appeal on human rights grounds[17]; and

(3) Finally, for a limited number of cases where, for example, there may be an issue about the length of residence as seen in the previous chapter the time spent pending in-time appeal will count towards lawful residence for the purposes of this Rule.

Two examples of where the acceptance of Human Rights Claims (and therefore a right of appeal against refusal) have proven crucial spring to mind;

(a) Firstly, the raft of mostly previous students having been accused of obtaining English language certificates through the use of a Proxy[18]. Many of these individuals toiled for many years seeking to clear their names and obtain justice. The decision of the Court of Appeal in *Ahsan v The Secretary of State for the Home Department* [2017] EWCA Civ 2009 accepting that a human rights claim could arise provided a crucial remedy for many individuals in these circumstances. Many of those faced with such allegations were able to make applications allowing them to be treated as having accrued 10 years' lawful residence.

(b) Secondly, in similar circumstances, many previously highly skilled workers were accused of either having deceived the home office in respect of claimed income or having made false representations to HMRC in respect of their income for the purposes of their liability to pay tax. Many such individuals found that having applied for indefinite leave to remain under

---

[17] See, for example *TZ (Pakistan) and PG (India) v The Secretary of State for the Home Department* [2018] EWCA Civ 1109.

[18] Referred to as the ETS TOEIC scandal.

the applicable route (under the points-based system) any refusal would not attract a right of appeal; their sole basis of challenge was on Public Law grounds (Rationality, Illegality and Procedural Impropriety) rather than a fact-based challenge which would form part of a Statutory appeal. Those, however, who were able to demonstrate a claim to 10 years' residence were able to apply/vary pending applications into the long residence route. This meant that refusals attracted a statutory right of appeal and entitled the aggrieved to a fact-based challenge. Unlike in a Judicial Review where they would have to prove, for example, that the decision was one that could not have been rationally taken on the material before the decision-maker a statutory appeal entitled them to argue that the decision was simply wrong on the facts. Many applicants were able to establish their innocence and therefore entitlement to indefinite leave to remain under the long residence route. Had no statutory right of appeal existed it is unlikely that such an outcome could have been achieved.

We have seen, therefore, that it is usually best practice to apply to vary an outstanding application in the circumstances of the requisite period of lawful residence being accrued at a time when an in-time application is pending.

We will now consider a variation of those circumstances, namely where the requisite period is accrued after the decision on the application has been made but whilst an appeal is pending.

Application refused but appeal pending

The ability to succeed in these circumstances also demonstrates the importance of entitlement to a statutory right of appeal.

As can be seen from the facts in *MU Bangladesh* (above) it is entirely possible for an individual to accrue the necessary period of lawful residence whilst an appeal is pending. In that case the period was accrued whilst an appeal was pending before the equivalent of the Upper Tribunal (Immigration and Asylum Chamber) (UT) but there is no reason why this would not be possible whilst a Statutory appeal is pending before the Court of Appeal (Civil Division) (CA) or the Supreme Court (SC).

As mentioned briefly above, this statutory extension would not extend to challenges against the decisions of the UT, which arise only in the Administrative Court. This scenario will be considered in further detail in chapter eight below.

The correct process to follow in such cases will depend on a number of facts so each case must be considered on merit and the facts taken into account. The below simply sets out principles of general application and should not be considered to be prescriptive. The importance of considering the relevant facts of each case cannot be overstated.

Scenario 1 – if an appeal is pending and a claim to an entitlement to indefinite leave to remain has <u>already</u> been made and rejected (giving rise to a right of appeal) then an applicant need do nothing, but it is good practice to inform the Tribunal and Respondent that on the modified chronology (i.e. the one adopted by the Respondent in the refusal or an otherwise correct chronology) the relevant period of lawful residence has now been accrued and that the appeal can/should be allowed on that basis. Notifying the Respondent of this in advance may give the Respondent sufficient time to review and withdraw the decision with a view to granting leave to remain. Failing this, the Tribunal can reach an independent decision on entitlement to leave[19].

See chapter seven below for advice on how to approach an offer from the Secretary of State to withdraw or reconsider any decision.

Scenario 2 – an appeal is pending but no claim to entitlement had previously been made. In the circumstances it is likely that entitlement under **paragraph 276B** will be considered a 'new matter' for the purposes of **s 85** of the **2002 Act.** In these circumstances action will need to be taken by the applicant. They will need to, as above, notify the Respondent and Tribunal to their entitlement to leave to remain AND ask the Respondent to either grant leave to remain on the basis of the accrual or, failing that, give consent for the FtT to be able to consider this issue. If consent is given, the limitation in **s 85** (from the consideration of a new matter) will not apply.

Scenario 3 – in any event, if the refusal under challenge was accompanied by a requirement to state any additional grounds for remaining in the United Kingdom (one-stop notice) it is always advisable to file such a statement (statement of additional grounds (SAG)) notwithstanding (or in addition to) any of the advice above. The importance of responding to a one-stop notice can be illustrated by the decision in *Hydar (s. 120 response, s. 85 "new matter", Birch)* [2021] UKUT 176 (IAC) but its application may have a limited scope where a human rights claim has already been made. As such a more detailed and nuanced approach to the existing caselaw will be required. That is something that is outside of the scope of this book. Generally speaking, however, the making of a SAG in response to the one-stop

---

[19] See, for example *OA and Others (human rights; 'new matter'; s.120 : Nigeria)* [2019] UKUT 65 (IAC)

notice is always advisable as it protects an applicant's position even if that SAG does not immediately result in a reconsideration.

Scenario 4 – if none of the above result in the achieved outcome, one further remedy may be to withdraw any pending appeal and simply make a fresh application. Such an application, if made promptly, should afford the applicant the protection of **Paragraph 39E** of the Rules but carries a great risk – the bringing to an end the period of lawful residence. For this reason this approach should only be taken with the express understanding of the applicant that any negative decision on the subsequent application will not revive statutory leave and the applicant will be deemed an 'overstayer'[20].

None of the above is prescriptive and each situation will need to be considered on the merits. It may be the case that in any one case more than one of the suggested actions above may be necessary. Whether or not this is the case will depend upon the facts.

We have considered the situation for those applicants who were able to apply for leave to remain prior to the expiry of leave (in-time) and accrued the necessary period of residence whilst that application was pending. The next chapter considers those whose applications were made after the expiry of leave (overstayers).

---

[20] Indeed they will have been an overstayer (a person that requires leave to remain but no longer has it) from the moment their appeal rights had been exhausted, but by virtue of **paragraph 39E** are excluded from mandatory refusal on the basis of that overstaying if the subsequent application is made within the time-limit set out in the Rule.

CHAPTER SIX

APPLICATIONS BY OVERSTAYERS

In the previous chapter we considered the situation for those who had accrued 10 years' lawful residence during the currency of an application. This included consideration of what to do in the circumstances of an in-time application being made under a different route and then varied into the long residence route when the required period of residence is satisfied. We also considered the application of **paragraph 39E** in excluding treatment of the applicant as an 'overstayer'.

In this chapter we will consider the distinct question of whether **paragraph 39E** can be used to allow an applicant to accrue the required period of residence.

The short answer is "no".

Before explaining this, it is worth outlining the situation in which such an argument may arise:

Example 1

Person A entered the United Kingdom on XX-MM-2012.

Person A extended leave in-time so that leave was lawfully extended until YY-MM-2022 (YY-MM-2022 being more than 30 or more days[21] prior to XX-MM-2022 i.e. the date on which Person A would have accrued 10 years' lawful residence).

The day after expiry of leave (so at least 29 days prior to the accrual of 10 years' lawful residence) Person A expires for indefinite leave to remain under paragraph 276B. In their covering letter[22] Person A pleads reliance upon **paragraph 39E** claiming that the exemption from treatment as an overstayer can be used to cover the shortfall in leave, essentially extending leave whilst the application is pending in the same way in which the statutory extension above exists.

This may seem, on the face of it, a remarkable argument but such an interpretation was supported by other documentation and even the Secretary of State's own practice for many years. Indeed, a variation of this interpretation was accepted by a minority Judgment in the Court of Appeal as we will see below.

This argument has been considered by the Senior Courts on multiple occasions, each Court reaching the same conclusions from a slightly different path.

First came the decision of the Upper Tribunal (Immigration and Asylum Chamber) in *Ahmed, R (on the application of) v Secretary of State for the Home Department (para 276B – ten years lawful residence)* [2019] UKUT 10. The decision in this case was made primarily on the basis of statutory interpretation (or more strictly, interpretation of the rules).

The applicant before the Upper Tribunal – Juned Ahmed (JA) – entered the United Kingdom in October 2006. Based on the chronology set out within the decision it would appear that JA had

---

[21] The significance of this period will be addressed further below

[22] Applications should always be accompanied by a covering letter setting out

leave to remain until the 22nd of January 2016. On the 4th of February 2016 i.e. 13 days after the expiry of leave to remain he made an application under a route other than long residence. He attempted to vary that application in March 2016. It is unclear why that variation was not considered, and the Secretary of State refused the first application in July 2016.

JA sought to challenge that decision and the challenge was subsequently settled, with the consequence that the Secretary of State was consider a second variation (originally applied for in September 2016 – so after the decision on the first application had been made) as stemming from the original application made in February 2016.

In the September 2016 variation JA relied upon paragraph 276B to establish an entitlement to indefinite leave to remain under the long residence route.

That varied application was considered, refused and the resultant human rights claim certified as unfounded. JA therefore brought a challenge by way of Judicial Review proceedings.

The (alternative) principle argument in that case was that **paragraph 276B(v)** (the requirement that an individual not be in the United Kingdom in breach of immigration rules (i.e. as an overstayer) unless **paragraph 39E** applies) could be used in the circumstances such as those in which Person A (in the example above) finds themselves.

The argument was that if **paragraph 276B(v)** applied to a period of overstaying, that period was not only to be disregarded as a breach of immigration rules but also to be treated as a period during which the applicant had leave to remain [45].

The Tribunal held, in summary, that the Rule could not properly be interpreted in such a way as to mean that a person such as Person A (above) could succeed[23] [75]. It would appear that the interpretation of the Rule was considered in isolation without any reference to the guidance.

Next came the decision of the Court of Appeal in *Ahmed, R (on the application of) v The Secretary of State for the Home Department* [2019] EWCA Civ 1070. Although the surname of the Appellant in this case is the same as that in the Judicial Review decision we have just considered, the two cases do not involve the same party.

In this case the Appellant Masum Ahmed (MA) had, by the time of his first application for indefinite leave to remain (made on the 16th of January 2016), been in the United Kingdom for around 10 years and 5 months, except for a trip to Bangladesh in December 2006 from which he returned in February 2007.

He had established roughly 3 years and 4 months of continuous lawful residency prior to his trip to Bangladesh which was made at a time when he still had leave to remain but by the time of his return to the United Kingdom that previous leave had expired.

MA went on to make two out of time applications for leave to remain (one having been rejected as invalid) before being granted a further period of leave to remain. These applications were made in February and September 2007. The September 2007 application resulted in a grant of leave to remain (roughly 8 months' leave to remain).

Following the expiry of that further period of leave to remain MA made another out of time application for further leave to remain, which was successful and the resultant leave was extant (i.e. still in

---

[23] The facts in *Ahmed* meant that the legal challenge was actually against the decision to certify the claim as unfounded which means that technically the finding from the Upper Tribunal was that the argument advanced was lawfully certified as unfounded.

place) until MA's subsequent first application for indefinite leave to remain on the basis of Long Residence.

The refusal of that application was subject to reconsiderations and appeals ultimately resulting in MA's appeal rights becoming exhausted almost four years later.

MA then made his second application for indefinite leave to remain on the basis of long residence; the application being made 8 days after the expiry of any appeal rights (on the 29th of December 2017). This application was varied into a different category once, and then varied back to being an application under the long residence rule. That application was considered, refused and certified as being unfounded.

In refusing the application the Secretary of State took issue with two 'gaps' in his period of continuous lawful residence (one in 2008 when MA's leave to remain had expired by the time of his successful application for further leave to remain and the second in 2016 between the expiry of leave to remain through appeal rights being exhausted and the second application for indefinite leave to remain).

MA sought to challenge that certification (and therefore the refusal of indefinite leave to remain) by way of proceedings for Judicial Review.

The principal argument from MA was that both 'gaps' identified above were of a sufficiently short period to be covered by **paragraph 276B(v)** (and therefore **paragraph 39E**) and that therefore should be disregarded for the purposes of his application and entitle him to leave to remain.

The Court rejected that argument essentially finding that (i) paragraph 276B(v) entitles the decision-maker to disregard both current and previous periods of overstaying which fall within the 'grace period' [15(4)]; but (ii) that 'disregard' entitlement does not convert that period of overstaying into periods of lawful residence [15(5)].

Next in this particular line of cases came the Court of Appeal's decision in *Hoque* (see above). That appeal concerns four appellants.

Each of the three Appellants had one broad similarity in their immigration histories; each had made an application for leave to remain (or indefinite leave to remain) at a time when they were overstayers protected by virtue of **paragraph 276B(v)**.

The court identified the following issues to be resolved, per Underhill LJ:

'[20] The essential elements in the situations of these three Appellants which give rise to the issue before us are as follows:

(1) their last period of limited leave expired before they had accumulated ten years' continuous lawful residence;

(2) they did not make any further application prior to the expiry of that leave, so as to attract the operation of section 3C of the 1971 Act, and accordingly became overstayers at that point;

(3) they made a further application for leave within 14 days (in the case of Mr Arif and Mr Kabir) or 28 days (in the case of Mr Hoque) of the expiry of the earlier leave, which was in due course varied so as to become an application for ILR;

(4) that varied application was pending at the tenth anniversary of their arriving in the UK but was subsequently refused.

These are all therefore cases of open-ended overstaying.'

To understand this reference to open-ended overstaying (as would become essential to understand a distinguishing feature between different types of overstaying that is necessary for the next decision we will consider) we have to turn to paragraphs 8 and 9 of the decision of Underhill LJ. Those paragraphs set the foundation for two important principles that will follow[24], they state the following:

'[8] Paragraph 276B provides (so far as material for our purposes):

"The requirements to be met by an applicant for indefinite leave to remain on the ground of long residence in the United Kingdom are that:

(i) (a)[1] he has had at least 10 years continuous lawful residence in the United Kingdom.

(ii) having regard to the public interest there are no reasons why it would be undesirable for him to be given indefinite leave to remain on the ground of long residence, ... and

(iii) the applicant does not fall for refusal under the general grounds for refusal.

(iv) the applicant has demonstrated sufficient knowledge of the English language and sufficient knowledge about life in the United Kingdom ... .

---

[24] Firstly the difference between the two types of overstaying and; flowing from that the way in which the Rule must be re arranged to be read properly.

(v) [A] the applicant must not be in the UK in breach of immigration laws, [B] except that, where paragraph 39E of these Rules applies, any current period of overstaying will be disregarded. [C] Any previous period of overstaying between periods of leave will also be disregarded where –

(a) the previous application was made before 24 November 2016 and within 28 days of the expiry of leave; or

(b) the further application was made on or after 24 November 2016 and paragraph 39E of these Rules applied."

I have inserted the letters [A]-[C] before each of the elements in sub-paragraph (v) so as to make subsequent reference to them easier.

[9] To anticipate, these appeals primarily focus on the effect of sub-paragraph (v) of paragraph 276B. I will have to analyse it more fully later, but at this stage it is important to note that it consists of the primary "requirement" ([A]), followed by provision for two circumstances in which periods of overstaying may be "disregarded" ([B] and [C]), the first of which relates to "*current* ... overstaying" and the second to "*previous* ... overstaying *between periods of leave*". Those two kinds of overstaying were referred to in the argument before us as, respectively, "open-ended" and "book-ended" overstaying. I should also explain that the distinction under element [C] based on the date of the previous/further application reflects the fact that as from 24 November 2016 the previous general policy under the Rules of disregarding periods of overstaying of under 28

days was abandoned and a regime providing for different kind of disregard ("the paragraph 39E regime") was introduced.'

Essentially at this stage of his Judgment Underhill LJ is simply setting out the relevant rule (with paragraph 276B(v) separated into three parts) and then explaining the two different types of overstaying:

(i)   Book-ended i.e. where the period of overstaying is both proceeded and preceded by a period of leave to remain; and

(ii) open-ended i.e. where the period of overstaying has not been proceeded by a subsequent grant of leave to remain.

The Court upheld the conclusions of both *Ahmed* decisions albeit finding that the reasoning in *MA* was incorrect on a discrete point and that the reasoning in *JA* was too broadly expressed [35, 45].

Interestingly in order to properly interpret the provisions within the rules Underhill LJ accepted that some 'violence' would have to be done to the drafting of the rules [44].

The violence that was done to the rule is explained as follows:

> '[35] It follows that we are faced with a choice between, on the one hand, giving element [C] no effect and, on the other, treating its placing within paragraph 276B as a drafting error and applying it as if it qualified sub-paragraph (i) (a). In my view we should choose the latter. It is unfortunately not uncommon for tribunals and courts to have to grapple with provisions of the Immigration Rules which are confusingly drafted, but it is our job to try to ascertain what the drafter intended to achieve and give effect to it so far as possible. In this case it is clear from its terms what the intended effect of element [C] is, but it has

been put in the wrong place. Treating it as if it appeared in sub-paragraph (i) (a) does violence to the drafting structure, but I do not believe that that is a sufficient reason not to give effect to it.'

The Rule can thus be reformulated as follows:

'The requirements to be met by an applicant for indefinite leave to remain on the ground of long residence in the United Kingdom are that:

(i)   (a)[11] he has had at least 10 years continuous lawful residence in the United Kingdom. Any previous period of overstaying between periods of leave will [also] be disregarded where –

     (a) the previous application was made before 24 November 2016 and within 28 days of the expiry of leave; or

     (b) the further application was made on or after 24 November 2016 and paragraph 39E of these Rules applied.

(ii) having regard to the public interest there are no reasons why it would be undesirable for him to be given indefinite leave to remain on the ground of long residence, ... and

(iii) the applicant does not fall for refusal under the general grounds for refusal.

(iv) the applicant has demonstrated sufficient knowledge of the English language and sufficient knowledge about life in the United Kingdom ... .

(v) the applicant must not be in the UK in breach of immigration laws, except that, where paragraph 39E of these Rules applies, any current period of overstaying will be disregarded.'

This interpretation was the foundation for the finding in the subsequent decision in *Asif (Paragraph 276B, disregard, previous overstaying) Pakistan* [2021] UKUT 96 (IAC).

In that case the Upper Tribunal (Upper Tribunal Judge Blum) began by summarising the decision of the Court of Appeal in *Hoque* in the following way:

'[1] A majority of the Court concluded that sub-paragraph 276B(i)(a), which requires an applicant to have had "at least 10 years continuous lawful residence", was to be read in conjunction with sub-paragraph 276B(v) which provides for a 'disregard' in respect of "any previous period of overstaying between periods of leave".'

The issue to be resolved by the Upper Tribunal was *'whether any "previous period of overstaying" that has been "disregarded" should be taken into account when determining whether an applicant has fulfilled the requirements for " 10 years continuous lawful residence."'* [2]

The facts of Asif concerned what the Court of Appeal had termed *"book-ended"* overstaying i.e. a period of overstaying bookended by periods of leave to remain. There was one further litigation feature distinguishing it from both *Ahmed* cases and all of the cases in *Hoque* which arose from proceedings for Judicial Review[25], the instant case

---

[25] One Appellant in Hoque (Mr Arif) had had a Statutory appeal but his application to the Court of Appeal had resulted from Judicial Review proceedings against the Upper Tribunal's decision to refuse permission to appeal.

resulted from a Statutory Appeal – therefore UTJ Blum was concerned not only with interpreting the law, but with applying it to the facts of the instant case on a fact-sensitive basis (i.e. not one focussed on the rationality of the Secretary of State's decision).

Ultimately, on consideration of the effect of the decision in *Hoque*, leaning heavily on the minority Judgment of McCombe LJ but also considering the effect of the Secretary of State's guidance, UTJ Blum found that for the purposes of book-ended overstaying the disregard provision does require the Secretary of State for the Home Department to treat the period as having been lawful residence.

As above, to reach his conclusion UTJ relied heavily on an interpretation of the guidance. The guidance is copied at paragraphs 8 and 9 of the Judgment, which states as follows:

'[8] The respondent's Long Residence Guidance, version 16, published on 28 October 2019 states, in material part:

Gaps in lawful residence

You may grant the application if an applicant:

- has short gaps in lawful residence through making previous applications out of time by no more than 28 calendar days where those gaps end before 24 November 2016

- has short gaps in lawful residence on or after 24 November 2016 but leave was granted in accordance with paragraph 39E of the Immigration Rules

- meets all the other requirements for lawful residence'

Although UTJ Blum quotes from the guidance dated 28 October 2019 version 16, the guidance has since been updated to version 17 published on the 11th of May 2021 (two months after the promulgation of the decision in *Asif*) and maintains the guidance as above[26].

Unfortunately this was far from being the final say in the matter. More fact-sensitive cases will be addressed in the following chapter but it would be remiss to end the current chapter without observing that UTJ Blum's decision and the reasoning leading to the conclusion were called into question by the Court of Appeal in *Afzal, R (On the Application Of) v Secretary of State for the Home Department* [2021] EWCA Civ 1909 and then subsequently in *Iyieke, R (On the Application Of) v Secretary of State for the Home Department* [2022] EWCA Civ 1147.

The position for now is that periods of open-ended overstaying will not count towards the continuous lawful residence required by **paragraph 276B(i)**, notwithstanding the protection from treatment as a person in breach of immigration rules set out in **paragraph 276B(v)**.

The position for those with book-ended overstaying is less clear, with UTJ Blum suggesting in *Asif* that it does count, Sir Patrick Elias suggesting in *Afzal* that this is incorrect (without expressly overruling it) [71-77] and that finding being upheld by Dingemans LJ in *Iyieke*, effectively overruling *Asif* even if *Afzal* had not expressly done so.

That understanding of the current position has to be understood with one major caveat; the Supreme Court has granted permission to appeal in the case of *Afzal* and so it is possible that the position in law changes on account of a subsequent decision of the Supreme Court.

---

[26] Long residence (publishing.service.gov.uk)

As mentioned variously throughout the preceding chapter, there has been much litigation involving the true construction and application of this particular rule. To gain a better understanding the following chapter will consider some other decisions of the Courts in this regard.

CHAPTER SEVEN

OTHER DECISIONS
OF THE COURTS

The decisions addressed in the previous chapter are primarily focussed on the issue of interpreting the rule. The fact that so much Court time has been spent on having to interpret what should be jargon-free simply-drafted Immigration Rules, has caused obvious discontent among the Judiciary.

Indeed it is worth quoting fully the post-script to Underhill LJ's Judgment in *Hoque*, as follows:

> '[59] This Court has very frequently in recent years had to deal with appeals arising out of difficulties in understanding the Immigration Rules. This is partly a result of their labyrinthine structure and idiosyncratic drafting conventions but sometimes it is a simple matter of the confused language and/or structure of particular provisions. This case is a particularly egregious example. The difficulty of deciding what the effect of paragraph 276B (v) is intended to be is illustrated by the facts not only that this Court itself is not unanimous but that all three members have taken a different view from that reached by a different constitution in *Masum Ahmed*. Likewise, the Secretary of State initially sought to uphold *Masum Ahmed* – contrary, it would seem to her own Guidance – but, as we have seen, shortly before the hearing executed a *volte face*. (This illustrates a different vice, also far from unique, that the Home Office seems to have no reliable mechanism for reaching a considered and

consistent position on what its own Rules mean.) Of course mistakes will occasionally occur in any complex piece of legislation, or quasi-legislation; but I have to say that problems of this kind occur too often. The result of poor drafting is confusion and uncertainty both for those who are subject to the Rules and those who have to apply them, and consequently also a proliferation of appeals. The Secretary of State has already taken a valuable first step towards improving matters by asking the Law Commission to report on the simplification of the Immigration Rules, and I hope that action will be taken on those recommendations. But the problem goes further than matters of structure and presentation, and I would hope that thought is also being given to how to improve the general quality of the drafting of the Rules.'

The entire paragraph is a rebuke to those responsible for the drafting of the rules as well as to those attempting to present the Secretary of State's interpretation of the rules given the reversal of their position.

It is also worth pointing out that since that Judgment the Court has revisited similar issues of interpretation on at least four occasions in *R(Akinola) v Upper Tribunal* [2021] EWCA Civ 1308', *Secretary of State for the Home Department v Ali* [2021] EWCA Civ 1357, and *R(Afzal) v Secretary of State for the Home Department* [2021] EWCA Civ 1909, and *Iyieke, R (On the Application Of) v Secretary of State for the Home Department* [2022] EWCA Civ 1147 ; the most recent of which was handed-down the month prior to completion of this book and stated that despite the Supreme Court being told that *"the Home Office are in the process of redrafting this section and attempting to simplify the rules overall"* in response to the application for permission to appeal in *Hoque*, Counsel for the Secretary of State was unable to inform the Court when this redrafting would take place [1].

In the remainder of this chapter we will consider some of those cases with reference to the more discrete findings contained within them.

Akinola

We begin with *Akinola*. We discussed in chapter four above, the effect of bringing an appeal in-time i.e. within the statutorily prescribed time-limit. One issue in *Akinola* was what effect it would have on continuous leave for an applicant to have brought an appeal out of time.

Following detailed consideration of the opposing arguments Sir Stephen Richards was persuaded that **section 3C** leave could be revived retrospectively if an out of time appeal is admitted (i.e. that the entire period from when the out of time appeal is lodged is deemed covered by **Section 3C(2)(a)** of the **Immigration Act 1971**) [64], see also [57].

The Court went on then to consider two other important categories; namely withdrawn decisions and those subject to reconsideration. The effect that these actions have on an applicant's leave to remain will depend upon the action being taken but when the features that distinguish the categories is properly understood the reason for the difference in effect will be clear.

Withdrawn decisions are those which the Secretary of State revokes or 'takes back' such that the decision is no longer in force. A comparison is drawn to decisions that are quashed by the Courts with the resultant submission from both parties pointing to the same outcome (a continuation or revival of statutorily extended leave) [65]-[67].

However on the basis of nuances in the approach the Court ultimately held that withdrawals will result in a revival or continuation of statutorily extended leave but only from the time of the decision to withdraw. This seems a bizarre finding; effectively that a decision which has been withdrawn (for any reason) has legal effect until the time of its withdrawal and is not considered a nullity as it would have been had a Court quashed it.

More will be said on this odd comparison below.

The second category was that of reconsiderations, defined by the Court as '[69] an internal review of the original decision'. The position here is easier to follow; a reconsideration (not resulting from a quashed or withdrawn decision) does not affect the legal status of the previous decision and therefore has no impact upon statutorily extended leave.

These findings lead us to an important point of practice in terms of advising clients; when the Secretary of State offers to withdraw a decision or reconsider and remake a decision, an advisor needs to ensure that the effect of the action being taken by the Secretary of State is clear and expressly set out.

For example if following Judicial Review proceedings the Secretary of State proposes a settlement in terms that requires a reconsideration of the decision, this may seem an attractive suggestion. However, following the finding in *Akinola* a mere reconsideration (without more) would not have the effect of negating the effect of the first decision (i.e. the one challenged in Judicial Review).

Applying the reasoning at [66] (dealing with the reason behind a withdrawal) even a withdrawal of the challenged decision may not be sufficient[27].

---

[27] Although, as recognised at the end of that paragraph the gap between the impugned decision and the ultimate withdrawal would be subject to discretion which <u>will</u> be exercised so that an applicant is not caused prejudice though withdrawal.

To be on the safe side, in these circumstances a variation of the following consent Order is suggested:

IN THE UPPER TRIBUNAL

IMMIGRATION AND ASYLUM CHAMBER

JR/2022/LON/XXXXX

THE KING ON THE APPLICATION OF

(NAME OF APPLICANT)

Applicant

V

THE SECRETARY OF STATE

FOR THE HOME DEPARTMENT (SSHD)

Respondent

BEFORE Upper Tribunal Judge XX

UPON the Respondent agreeing to withdraw the decision dated XX-MM-XX so that the application made on YY-MM-YY is neither decided nor withdrawn for the purposes of the Immigration Act 1971;

AND

UPON the Respondent expressly agreeing that the withdrawn decision of XX-MM-XX is to have no legal effect;

And

Upon the Respondent agreeing to consider the application of YY-YY-YY within three months (absent exceptional circumstances);

IT IS HEREBY ORDERED THAT

1) The Applicant have permission to withdraw this Claim for Judicial Review; and

2) The Respondent pay the Applicant's costs of bringing this claim to be assessed if not agreed.

Signed	Dated
Solicitor for the Applicant	Solicitor for the Respondent
Name	Name
Firm	Firm
Address	Address
Reference Number	Reference Number

Akter

A case that illustrates the importance of such an approach (i.e. one where offers to reconsider a previous decision should be accompanied by express statements that the previous decision would be considered quashed or, at least, have no legal effect) is *Akter, R (On the Application Of) v Secretary of State for the Home Department* [2021] EWCA Civ 704.

This case succeeded in the Court of Appeal on the basis that it was arguable that an application was not finally determined until a decision was made following reconsideration (which followed Judicial

Review proceedings). The hearing before the Court of Appeal was limited to considering whether permission to move for Judicial Review ought to have been granted (i.e. whether the Upper Tribunal were wrong in refusing permission to move for Judicial Review).

However when the matter was remitted to the Upper Tribunal for a substantive Judicial Review hearing it was successfully argued by the Secretary of State that the subsequent reconsidered decision did not replace the previous decision and even if it had, the earlier decision would have retained legal effect. In his Judgement in that case[28] UTJ O'Callaghan specifically referred to the fact that the Order by which earlier Judicial Review proceedings were settled does not have the effect of quashing the decision under challenge in those proceedings.

Ali

In the case of _Ali_ the applicant had successfully argued that an application to which **paragraph 39E** had applied (i.e. one that was made _after_ the expiry of leave but _within_ the grace period covered by **paragraph 39E**) should be treated as an 'in-time' application.

The effect of this argument was that when that application was refused the applicant made a fresh application within 14 days of that refusal (14 days being the period applicable under **paragraph 39E** at the time of the fresh application) the applicant was able to successfully argue (at the lower courts) that **paragraph 39E(2)** applied and he was therefore exempt from mandatory refusal as an overstayer.

The Court of Appeal rejected this argument and allowed the Secretary of State's appeal. In setting out her findings and reasons Simler LJ stated the following:

---

[28] Unreported

'[37] Once it is recognised that applications for leave to remain must (in general) be made before the expiry of a person's existing leave, and that this is the deadline within which such applications must (in general) be made if they are to be considered on their merits, it follows that an application made before expiry of the deadline is an "in-time" application, whereas an application made after the expiry of the deadline is *not* "in-time". The grace period (whether 14 or 28 days) disregard is different and distinct from the concept of an "in-time" application. An application made out of time but nevertheless within 28 days of expiry of an existing leave period, could not be refused merely because the application was not made "in-time". The 28 day grace period was an indulgence applied to *late* applications to ensure that where the lateness was relatively short and there was good reason for it, this would not operate as a ground for refusal in and of itself.'

It is therefore clear that the term 'in-time' means prior to the expiry of leave to remain and does not extend to cover those applications made once an individual's leave to remain has expired, even where that application was made within the grace period provided for within paragraph 39E.

The finding affects those in the following circumstances:

Example 2

Person B entered the United Kingdom on XX-MM-2012.

Person B extended leave in-time so that leave was lawfully extended until YY-MM-2021.

On YY+1 – MM – 2021 Person B applies for leave to remain (first application). That application is one day after the expiry of leave to remain so is covered by the exception to mandatory refusal, by virtue of **paragraph 39E**.

Following the refusal of that application Person B makes a fresh application (second application) within 14 days (the period currently applicable under **paragraph 39E**).

That application is refused on the basis that Person B's second application was made more than 14 days after the refusal of an in-time application and therefore the second application cannot rely on **paragraph 39E**.

In the above scenario, Person B has no proper challenge to the refusal on the basis of overstaying because the first application is not an *in-time* application for the purposes of **paragraph 39E** and so that paragraph cannot be invoked in the second application. This is the case even if Person B were able to satisfy all other requirements of the Rules.

Let us contrast this with a person who had made an in-time application, as below:

Example 3

Person C entered the United Kingdom on XX-MM-2012.

Person C extended leave in-time so that leave was lawfully extended until YY-MM-2021.

On YY-1 – MM – 2021 Person C applies for leave to remain (first application). That application is one day prior to the expiry of leave to remain and so would engage the statutory extension under **s 3C** of the **Immigration Act 1971** if not decided prior to the expiry of leave to remain.

Following the refusal of that application and the expiry of any right to appeal or seek administrative review Person C makes a fresh application (second application) within 14 days.

That application is successful on the basis that Person C's second application was made within 14 days of the refusal of an in-time application and therefore the second application does rely on **paragraph 39E**[29].

We can now see that two individuals in almost identical scenarios, except that one unsuccessfully applied prior to the expiry of leave (Person C) and the other unsuccessfully applied after the expiry of leave (Person B) have very different outcomes to their second applications; even if both satisfied the other requirements of the rules.

This is illustrative of the importance of maintaining the continuity of leave to remain (even through the exercise of the Statutory extension) wherever possible. In the next two chapters we will consider circumstances in which either this is not possible or other exemptions may apply and situations in which the continuity of leave will be broken (rather than the lawfulness of leave as covered by the current and previous chapters).

---

[29] Of course the basis of success of the second application would also be that Person C satisfied the requirements of the rules.

CHAPTER EIGHT

BREAKS IN CONTINUITY

The next two chapters will address primarily the long residence guidance. This chapter will address how the guidance informs the interpretation of the 'continuous' requirement in continuous lawful residence and the next chapter will address any discretion provided for within the guidance.

The guidance lists the following events that break the continuity of residence:

'Events that break continuous residence

Continuous residence is considered to be broken if the applicant has:

- been absent from the UK for a period of more than 6 months at any one time

- spent a total of 18 months outside the UK throughout the whole 10 year period

- left the UK before 24 November 2016 with no valid leave to remain on their departure from the UK, and failed to apply for entry clearance within 28 days of their previous leave expiring (even if they returned to the UK within 6 months)'

The application of this guidance can be seen through the example below:

Example 4

Person D leaves the United Kingdom whilst still having leave to remain endorsed on their visa.

They return to their Country of Nationality and apply to re-enter the United Kingdom as the spouse of a person present and settled in the United Kingdom and are granted entry clearance. They return to the United Kingdom within 6 months of their departure.

Person D's continuous lawful residence would not be broken in those circumstances as they would be able to establish that they had leave to remain both when they left the United Kingdom and when they returned (for these purposes leave to remain in a different Category is sufficient to maintain continuity[30]) and they were only outside of the United Kingdom for a period under six months in total.

The continuity would also remain intact if Person D had returned to their Country of origin after the expiry of leave to remain, provided that the period of overstaying was before 24 November 2016 and for fewer than 28 days. Person D would also have to establish that an entry clearance application was made within 28 of their previous leave expiring and that they re-entered the United Kingdom within 6 months of departure.

Another provision regarding departure from the United Kingdom requires that an Applicant not have been absent from the United

---

[30] The guidance expressly confirms that entry under the EEA Regulations would also be counted towards this continuity. For more information on the position for those with residence rights under the Regulations see the following chapter.

Kingdom for more than 18 months[31] in the relevant 10-year period unless 'compelling or compassionate circumstances' apply.

Examples of such circumstances could include medical emergency or documented inability to travel on medical grounds, the shut-down of global travel due to a pandemic or the eruption of an Icelandic volcano causing delays in travel, for example. The guidance document sets a high threshold requiring a situation 'where the applicant was prevented from returning to the UK through unavoidable circumstances'.

The guidance set out the following instructions to decision-makers:

'Things to consider when assessing if the absence was compelling or compassionate are:

- for all cases – you must consider whether the individual returned to the UK within a reasonable time once they were able to do so

- for the single absence of over 180 days:

  o you must consider how much of the absence was due to compelling circumstances and whether the applicant returned to the UK as soon as they were able to do so

  o you must also consider the reasons for the absence

- for overall absences of 540 days in the 10 year period:

  o you must consider whether the long absence (or absences) that pushed the applicant over the limit

---

[31] Defined as '30 calendar days'

happened towards the start or end of the 10 year residence period, and how soon they will be able to meet that requirement

o if the absences were towards the start of that period, the person may be able to meet the requirements in the near future, and so could be expected to apply when they meet the requirements

o however, if the absences were recent, the person will not qualify for a long time, and so you must consider whether there are particularly compelling circumstances

All of these factors must be considered together when determining whether it is reasonable to exercise discretion.'

It will be evident that in addition to the high threshold, there is also a requirement that an applicant establish that they took remedial action promptly. There also seems to be a balancing exercise to be undertaken by a decision-maker including whether the applicant may be able to qualify in the near future without needing to take into account the absence.

The final category of those by whom continuity of leave may be broken is those who have been sentenced to a term of imprisonment. The guidance document includes the following under this term:

'Continuous residence is broken if an applicant receives a custodial sentence by a court of law and is sent to:

• prison

• a young offender institution

• a secure hospital'

It goes onto to state that not only will that period of imprisonment be disregarded, it will also cause *'[a]ny leave accumulated before sentencing will be disregarded and only residence after release from custody will be counted as continuous residence.'*

It could certainly be argued that such an approach could constitute a disproportionate response to offending. For example:

Example 5

Person E has accrued nine years of continuous lawful residence in the United Kingdom.

Person E is a person of previously good character but two months prior to accruing 10 years' lawful residence Person E is sentenced to a term of imprisonment of one week

Person E would not only find their leave to remain in the United Kingdom broken by the one-week term of imprisonment, they would also be disqualified from obtaining indefinite leave to remain in this category for another ten years.

Although the guidance is silent as to discretion under this particular element, it is clear that discretion exists in relation to breaks in continuity generally and as will be seen below there is also discretion in other regards, so one would hope for a sympathetic decision-maker able to exercise discretion in favour of Person E to avoid such a disproportionate response to their imprisonment.

One example of a situation in which discretion is exercised without being set out in the guidance relates to those individuals accused of having fraudulently obtained English language certificates (the ETS TOEIC scandal, see chapter five above). Following the decision of the Court in *Ahsan* and subsequent decision of the Court of Appeal in

Khan & Ors v Secretary of State for the Home Department [2018] EWCA Civ 1684 many individuals were able to settle pending claims on the basis that if, following a fact-sensitive appeal hearing, they were able to establish that the allegation against them had not been proven the Secretary of State would treat any period following the unfounded allegation of deception as having been on the same status as prior to the allegation being made.

Thus many who would have had leave but for the allegation (often made in a removal decision or a curtailment of existing leave) were able to establish their innocence many years later and have that entire period considered as continuous lawful residence.

Of course, whether such agreement was possible with the Secretary of State depended on the facts of each individual case but it is unfortunate that only a limited number of individuals had the foresight to have such an expression set out in the Order by which proceedings were brought to an end.

This highlights again the importance of detailing all elements of the agreement within the draft Order sent to the Court or Tribunal for approval.

The following modified recital in cases of this nature would be suggested to the consent Order in Chapter 7 above:

UPON it being agreed between the Parties that if the allegation of deception is not made out before the Tribunal then the Applicant will be put back in the position (s)he was in before the allegation was originally made on DD-MM-YY. Any time thereafter will therefore be treated as if the Applicant's leave as it stood on DD-MM-YY remained extant.

Other examples of discretion contained within the guidance are set out in the following chapter.

There is one aspect that is yet to be addressed; what happens when a decision of the Upper Tribunal causes appeal rights to be exhausted but that decision is successfully challenged by way of Judicial Review proceedings.

This situation can only arise in a very narrow set out circumstances; the Upper Tribunal has refused permission to appeal from a decision of the FtT[32]. Such a decision can only be challenged by way of Judicial Review (see *Cart v The Upper Tribunal* [2011] UKSC 28).

Ultimately, when such a claim is successful the appeal becomes pending again for the purposes of the 2002 Act (see *Saimon (Cart Review: "pending" : Bangladesh)* [2017] UKUT 371 (IAC)). In *Niaz (NIAA 2002 s. 104: pending appeal) Pakistan* [2019] UKUT 399 (IAC) the following was stated:

'(3) An appeal which has ceased to be pending within the meaning of section 104 becomes pending again if the Upper Tribunal's decision refusing permission to appeal from the First-tier Tribunal is quashed on judicial review.'

---

[32] Other decisions of the UT are amenable to statutory appeal so would not have the effect of exhausting leave to remain (in the same way).

CHAPTER NINE

DISCRETION

In certain circumstances an individual who is/was unable to maintain the LAWFUL continuity of their leave to remain for the entire 10-year period may be able to avail themselves of discretion set out within the decision-maker's guidance.

The Relevant section of the guidance begins as follows:

> '**Breaks in lawful residence**
>
> This page tells you about circumstances that break lawful residence for long residence applications and when you can use discretion for short breaks in lawful residence.'

Before getting into the detail about breaks in lawful residence it is worth exploring an example of a situation where discretion will be exercised for those who have been granted residence under the relevant **European Economic Area Regulations** (the Regulations) prior to the route for qualified European Nationals and their family members being incorporated into the **Immigration Rules** through the **European Union Settlement Scheme**).

Individuals having been granted residence under the Regulations to apply under **paragraph 276B** would technically be unable to satisfy the requirement for continuous leave to remain; residence under the Regulations not being considered leave to remain.

In relation to applicants in these circumstances, the guidance states the following:

> 'Time spent in the UK does not count as lawful residence under paragraph 276A of the Immigration Rules for third country nationals who have spent time in the UK as: • the spouse, civil partner or other family member of a European Union (EU) national • an EEA national exercising their treaty rights to live in the UK but have not qualified for permanent residence • former family members who have retained a right of residence During the time spent in the UK under the provisions of the EEA regulations, the individuals are not subject to immigration control, and would not be required to have leave to enter or leave to remain. See EEA Nationals guidance for further information.'

Thankfully the guidance does go on to mandate the exercise of discretion in favour of such individuals:

> 'However, you must apply discretion and count time spent in the UK as lawful residence for an EU or EEA national or their family members exercising their treaty rights to reside in the UK. Sufficient evidence must be provided to demonstrate that the applicant has been exercising treaty rights throughout any period that they are seeking to rely on for the purposes of meeting the long residence rules.'

An example of circumstances in which this would be helpful is as below:

Example 6

Person F entered the United Kingdom on XX-MM-2012.

Person F had leave to remain until YY-MM-2020. On that day Person F was granted a residence card the under Regulations (non-EUSS).

On XX-MM-2022 Person F applies for indefinite leave to remain under **paragraph 276B.** That application is successful on the basis that although Person F has only ~8 years' continuous lawful residence for the purposes of the **Immigration Rules,** the remainder of the requisite period was time spent whilst Person F had been granted residence under the Regulations; discretion was exercised in favour of Person F.

This example is also illustrative of circumstances in which an application under **paragraph 276B** may be preferable to one under **Appendix EU** (EUSS); making the former application entitled Person F to indefinite leave to remain whereas under the latter Person F would have been granted limited leave to remain (pre-Settled Status). Person F would have been required to establish 5 years' residence (exercise of Treaty Rights) in order to qualify for indefinite leave to remain under EUSS[33].

This situation covers those who were successful in applications under the Regulations and subsequently granted leave. There are, however, two categories for whom difficulties will arise based on applications under the Regulations; (1) those who had applied under routes for which there is no direct effect (e.g. other (extended) family members); and (2) those who were unsuccessful in their application.

For the first category *Macastena v Secretary of State for the Home Department* [2018] EWCA Civ 1558 makes it clear that an entitlement to residence and therefore the relevant period of lawful residence only begins when an application under the Regulations was successful. If the applicant had leave to remain prior to the grant of residence under the Regulations then that previous grant should be

---

[33] Albeit in the case of direct effect rights, Person F may have been able to qualify under EUSS sooner for example if Person F was the family member of a qualified EU National from 2017 but only obtained the Residence Card in 2020, Person F may have acquired permanent residence under the Regulations and therefore an entitlement to the same under EUSS.

sufficient to be considered continuous residence. But many who had applied, for example, as unmarried partners did so following the expiry of any previous leave and therefore the application was made as an overstayer. In those circumstances the applicant could not avail him/herself of a grant of residence in order to make any previous period (including that during which the relationship was formed) count towards the requisite period of lawful residence.

In relation to the second category, similarly to if they held leave to remain at the time of the application and refusal, that leave to remain would be sufficient to cover that specific period (until the actual expiry of leave).

The difficulty arises for those who had applied in-time but the application was not considered until the expiry of leave to remain; they received no protection from **S 3C** of the **Immigration Act 1971**. Those individuals will find themselves treated as overstayers possibly for the period during which the application was being considered (discretion may be exercised in their favour not to do so) but certainly from the point of refusal.

There is a valid argument that the failure to provide protection for individuals in these circumstances is a breach of the United Kingdom's duties under the European Union principle of equivalence. Such an argument was rejected by the Upper Tribunal in *Ali & Ors v Secretary of State for the Home Department (EU Law equivalence)* [2022] UKUT 278 (IAC) with reference to *Totel Ltd v Revenue and Customs* [2018] UKSC 44 and *AS (Ghana) v Secretary of State for the Home Department* [2016] EWCA Civ 133 but is yet to be tested by the superior Courts.

The guidance applies the same approach to Turkish Nationals who have spent time in the United Kingdom under the ECAA:

'Time spent in the UK as a Turkish national whilst working under the ECAA worker provisions

A Turkish national may have spent time working in the UK under the ECAA provisions. Any time spent in the UK under this provision may be counted as legal continuous residence and count towards the 10 year qualifying period for leave under long residence.'

Another example of a situation in which discretion can be exercised in favour of a grant of leave to remain is the situation in which an individual applies early and their application is being considered within 28 days of the Applicant accruing the requisite period of leave.

The guidance states as follows:

'**Applications being considered 28 days or less before the required qualifying period is completed**

You can grant an application if it is considered 28 days or less before the applicant completes the required qualifying period, provided they meet all the other rules for long residence.'

However this guidance has to be interpreted carefully. Technically, the chronology of some of the Appellants in *Hoque* (above) satisfied this provision and indeed the guidance is referred to (though not cited) at [17(4)][34].

It appears that although the guidance is referred to none of the parties took the Court through the detail (see [91]) and so the question of

---

[34] Mr Hoque had varied his application such that he was seeking ILR within 28 days of the 10-year anniversary of his entry [17(4)] as did Mr Arif [19(4)]

whether an application being considered within 28 days of the accrual of 10 years' continuous lawful residence being allowed in line with the guidance has not been resolved albeit, at least two of the four Appellants in *Hoque* would have succeeded had the Court been persuaded by this particular argument.

Although reference is made to Secretary of State considering applications based on the facts prevailing at the date of decision (see [17(4)]) if that were the case and the guidance were applied (per *Pokhriyal* an applicant is entitled to ask a Court or Tribunal to hold the Secretary of State to an assurance of a lenient approach as set out in guidance[35]) at least two of the Appellants in *Hoque* ought to have succeeded.

It would appear, although this remains untested, that the basis for not applying the guidance would be one or both of the following:

(i)   The gap between the date of the application (i.e. the date on which the original application that engaged paragraph 39E was made) and the eventual 10-year anniversary; and/or

(ii) The gap between the date of the application and the date of the variation.

The following examples can be given:

---

[35] Similar points regarding an applicant's proper reliance upon guidance have been made in other cases including *Mandalia v Secretary of State for the Home Department* [2015] UKSC 59

Example 7

Person G applies for leave to remain within 14 days of the expiry of their previous visa (application).

Whilst that application is being considered Person G recognises that they will accrue 10 years' lawful residence within 28 days and therefore varies their application to one seeking Indefinite leave to remain under **paragraph 276B** (variation).

One would imagine that if the application was within the 28-day period the applicant could successfully rely upon the guidance. Similarly, if the variation was within the 14-day period under **paragraph 39E** it is likely[36] that the Secretary of State would apply the guidance and allow the variation and grant ILR.

The difficulty, it seems, for the Appellants in Hoque was that although the application was within the grace period, the variation was not. This approach, however, is inconsistent with the stated approach of the Secretary of State in making decisions based on the date of the decision rather than the date of the application.

Based on the decision in *Hoque* it would seem that the only situation in which an overstayer may be able to avail themselves of the early application concession is if that application is made within the grace period and at the time of making the application the applicant is within the 28-day concession period of their 10-year anniversary.

A final category of discretion is where either applications or appeals are lodged out of time (although the guidance deals with each situation separately). As was seen in the previous chapter the guidance

---

[36] Albeit untested at present

provides discretion where an individual was unable to return to the United Kingdom within the requisite timeframe.

Similarly, there is express discretion to disregard periods of overstaying of more than 28 days if before the 24th of November 2016.

The guidance states the following:

> 'When refusing an application on the grounds it was made by an applicant who has overstayed by more than 28 days, you must consider any evidence of exceptional circumstances which prevented the applicant from applying within the first 28 days of overstaying.
>
> The threshold for what constitutes 'exceptional circumstances' is high, but could include delays resulting from unexpected or unforeseeable causes. For example:
>
> • serious illness which meant the applicant or their representative was not able to submit the application in time – this must be supported by appropriate medical documentation
>
> • travel or postal delays which meant the applicant or their representative was not able to submit the application in time
>
> • inability to provide necessary documents – this would only apply in exceptional or unavoidable circumstances beyond the applicant's control, for example: o it is the fault of the Home Office because it lost or delayed returning travel documents o there is a delay because the applicant cannot replace their documents quickly because of theft, fire or flood – the applicant must send evidence of the date of loss and the date replacement

documents were sought Any decision to exercise discretion and not refuse the application on these grounds must be authorised by a senior caseworker at senior executive officer (SEO) grade or above. When granting leave in these circumstances, the applicant must be granted leave outside the rules for the same duration and conditions that would have applied had they been granted leave under the rules.'

In these circumstances the individual is granted leave to remain outside of the **Immigration Rules** but on the same conditions as would have applied under the rules.

The situation is slightly different for overstaying if after 24 November 2016. On that, the guidance states as follows:

'Where an out of time application is submitted on or after 24 November 2016, you must consider whether to exercise discretion in line with paragraph 39E of the immigration rules. This must be authorised by a senior caseworker at senior executive officer (SEO) grade.'

Finally dealing with the situation applicable to those who had appealed out of time (OoT), the guidance states the following in relation to the exercise of discretion:

'[y]ou should normally use discretion to disregard the break in continuous lawful residence immediately prior to the Tribunal granting permission to proceed where one of the following apply:

- the OoT appeal was subsequently allowed

- the OoT appeal was subsequently dismissed but further leave was granted following a further application made:

o within 28 days of 3C leave expiring where the application was made before the 24 November 2016

o after 24 November 2016 in accordance with paragraph 39E Any discretion on this basis will result in a grant outside of the Immigration Rules.'

It will again be seen that despite the concession, the application would not technically be successful under the immigration rules but rather outside of the rules as set out in the guidance.

The guidance also contains information on how to resolve an individual's status for any time that they were not subject to immigration control (for example in the United Kingdom under diplomatic powers) as well as how personal circumstances ought to be considered.

The situation for those not subject to immigration control is broadly that time spent in the United Kingdom with this status will count towards lawful residence. There will be slightly differently applicable rules on how long after the expiry of such status the individual is entitled to remain lawfully within in the United Kingdom but a question of that period would have to be considered on the facts (for example 90 days for diplomats and usually 28 days for former members of the armed forces following discharge).

We have now seen how the complex topics of continuity of leave and lawfulness of leave are considered under the rules. Those topics encompass the areas of focus of this book. There are, however, other requirements of the rules which will now be address in the following chapter.

CHAPTER TEN

OTHER CONSIDERATIONS

There are other requirements of the rules as set out above. Those broadly include the KOLL requirements, public interest or the application of the general grounds for refusal.

The knowledge of life in the UK requirement is proscriptive and self-explanatory. The topic of general grounds for refusal is complex and could be the subject of another book (or books) in itself.

The current chapter will briefly address any issues arising from the public interest requirement within **paragraph 276B(ii)**. The question is not aimed at establishing an applicant's entitlement to a grant of leave but rather whether any reasons exist why such leave should not be granted.

The final two categories of the public interest requirement, however, are aimed at rebutting any assertion that an applicant should not be granted leave to remain based on the preceding categories.

For example if an applicant's personal history suggested they ought not to be granted leave to remain, the Secretary of State is bound to consider any compassionate circumstances that exist and any representations that the applicant has put forward to respond to any assertion of bad character.

An important principle that follows from this approach is that the Secretary of State must make it plain that the public interest element is engaged and a refusal could follow.

The requirement to inform an applicant was made clear in the Judgment in *Balajigari v The Secretary of State for the Home Department* [2019] EWCA Civ 673 with the introduction of a "minded to refuse" procedure i.e. a procedure in which a decision-maker minded to refuse an application on character grounds invites a response from an applicant prior to making any decision.

This approach was firstly adopted in Nationality cases following the decision in *Fayed, R (on the application of) v Secretary Of State For Home Department* [1996] EWCA Civ 946 and the principle has since been extended to other categories within the rules too.

Such an approach would allow the decision-maker to reach a balanced decision, following (the opportunity for) proper representation by the applicant[37] taking into account all relevant factors.

A non-exhaustive list of examples in which an applicant's conduct may suggest a grant of leave is inappropriate are as follows:

> 'Character, conduct and associations go beyond criminal convictions and allow you to consider whether the applicant's activities in the UK, or abroad, makes it undesirable for you to grant indefinite leave.
>
> This could include concerns about the applicant on the basis of:
>
> • national security
>
> • war crimes
>
> • crimes against humanity

---

[37] An opportunity which an applicant should almost always take

- serious criminality, whether convicted or not

- other activities that make the applicant's presence in the UK not conducive to the public good Applicants who do not satisfy the general grounds within the Immigration Rules now face refusal under the rules for settlement. See general grounds for refusal for more information.'

The final bullet-point has been utilised by the Secretary of State to successfully lower the threshold of the type of behaviour required to engage such a refusal. As mentioned above, individuals accused of having misrepresented their income to either the Home Office in order to secure further leave to remain or HMRC to reduce their tax liability were often met with refusals under this bullet point. Indeed, the case of *Balajigari* is illustrative of its use in such circumstances.

In order to strike a balance the decision maker is required to consider both sides of the argument. The guidance requires the following:

'You must consider whether there are any compassionate circumstances that would weigh against refusal.

It is not possible to define all potential compassionate circumstances, but it might, depending on the circumstances, include:

- significant or serious illness

- frailty

- particularly difficult family circumstances

Compassionate circumstances are most likely to be relevant if the applicant has been here for long enough to qualify for indefinite leave, but there are other factors, such as criminal convictions or an adverse immigration history, that suggest a grant of indefinite leave might not be appropriate.'

As mentioned earlier, the existence of a statutory right of appeal is a vital resource when faced with a refusal. In a statutory appeal it would be open to an individual to invite a tribunal to conduct its own balancing exercise in deciding whether or not the decision is a proportionate interference with their human rights[38].

---

[38] This argument could also be deployed in a Judicial Review, but the UT maintains a reluctance (despite clear caselaw) to enter into the arena of fact-sensitive human rights Judicial Review claims.

CHAPTER ELEVEN

CONCLUSIONS

As above both the Superior Courts and the Law commission have expressed their views that the rules are in need of complete overhaul. In the case of the rule under consideration presently the difficulty in interpreting the rule compounded by poor drafting, arguably ambiguous statements within the guidance[39], inconsistent approach by those acting on behalf of the government and frankly a well-developed practice whereby decision-makers were previously granting applications in circumstances in which they would now refuse.

A reform of the rules is certainly required but the problem may run deeper; it seems the management of the entire system of immigration control is bursting at the seams and needs root and branch restructuring. There was, of course, the restructure from UKBA to UKVI, Border Force and Immigration Control in 2013[40] but that was ineffective in bringing any substantive change.

The problems run deeper than this one rule (to which reform has been promised for some time) and run to a departmental and perhaps even governmental level. Perhaps a radical new approach is required.

---

[39] Although Sir Patrick Elias found no ambiguity, UTJ Blum (an experienced UT Judge and previously highly regarded Immigration Barrister) did find ambiguity.

[40] UK Border Agency – GOV.UK (www.gov.uk)

MORE BOOKS BY
LAW BRIEF PUBLISHING

A selection of our other titles available now:-

'A Practical Guide to Parental Alienation in Private and Public Law Children Cases' by Sam King QC & Frankie Shama
'Contested Heritage – Removing Art from Land and Historic Buildings' by Richard Harwood QC, Catherine Dobson, David Sawtell
'The Limits of Separate Legal Personality: When Those Running a Company Can Be Held Personally Liable for Losses Caused to Third Parties Outside of the Company' by Dr Mike Wilkinson
'A Practical Guide to Transgender Law' by Robin Moira White & Nicola Newbegin
'Artificial Intelligence – The Practical Legal Issues (2nd Edition)' by John Buyers
'A Practical Guide to Residential Freehold Conveyancing' by Lorraine Richardson
'A Practical Guide to Pensions on Divorce for Lawyers' by Bryan Scant
'A Practical Guide to Challenging Sham Marriage Allegations in Immigration Law' by Priya Solanki
'A Practical Guide to Legal Rights in Scotland' by Sarah-Jane Macdonald
'A Practical Guide to New Build Conveyancing' by Paul Sams & Rebecca East
'A Practical Guide to Defending Barristers in Disciplinary Cases' by Marc Beaumont
'A Practical Guide to Inherited Wealth on Divorce' by Hayley Trim
'A Practical Guide to Practice Direction 12J and Domestic Abuse in Private Law Children Proceedings' by Rebecca Cross & Malvika Jaganmohan
'A Practical Guide to Confiscation and Restraint' by Narita Bahra QC, John Carl Townsend, David Winch
'A Practical Guide to the Law of Forests in Scotland' by Philip Buchan
'A Practical Guide to Health and Medical Cases in Immigration Law' by Rebecca Chapman & Miranda Butler
'A Practical Guide to Bad Character Evidence for Criminal Practitioners by Aparna Rao
'A Practical Guide to Extradition Law post-Brexit' by Myles Grandison et al

'A Practical Guide to Hoarding and Mental Health for Housing Lawyers'
by Rachel Coyle

'A Practical Guide to Psychiatric Claims in Personal Injury – 2nd Edition'
by Liam Ryan

'Stephens on Contractual Indemnities' by Richard Stephens

'A Practical Guide to the EU Succession Regulation' by Richard Frimston

'A Practical Guide to Solicitor and Client Costs – 2nd Edition' by Robin Dunne

'Constructive Dismissal – Practice Pointers and Principles' by Benjimin Burgher

'A Practical Guide to Religion and Belief Discrimination Claims in the Workplace'
by Kashif Ali

'A Practical Guide to the Law of Medical Treatment Decisions' by Ben Troke

'Fundamental Dishonesty and QOCS in Personal Injury Proceedings: Law and
Practice' by Jake Rowley

'A Practical Guide to the Law in Relation to School Exclusions'
by Charlotte Hadfield & Alice de Coverley

'A Practical Guide to Divorce for the Silver Separators' by Karin Walker

'The Right to be Forgotten – The Law and Practical Issues' by Melissa Stock

'A Practical Guide to Planning Law and Rights of Way in National Parks, the
Broads and AONBs' by James Maurici QC, James Neill et al

'A Practical Guide to Election Law' by Tom Tabori

'A Practical Guide to the Law in Relation to Surrogacy' by Andrew Powell

'A Practical Guide to Claims Arising from Fatal Accidents – 2nd Edition'
by James Patience

'A Practical Guide to the Ownership of Employee Inventions – From Entitlement
to Compensation' by James Tumbridge & Ashley Roughton

'A Practical Guide to Asbestos Claims' by Jonathan Owen & Gareth McAloon

'A Practical Guide to Stamp Duty Land Tax in England and Northern Ireland'
by Suzanne O'Hara

'A Practical Guide to the Law of Farming Partnerships' by Philip Whitcomb

'Covid-19, Homeworking and the Law – The Essential Guide to Employment and
GDPR Issues' by Forbes Solicitors

'Covid-19 and Criminal Law – The Essential Guide' by Ramya Nagesh

'Covid-19 and Family Law in England and Wales – The Essential Guide'
by Safda Mahmood

'A Practical Guide to the Law of Unlawful Eviction and Harassment – 2nd Edition' by Stephanie Lovegrove

'Covid-19, Brexit and the Law of Commercial Leases – The Essential Guide' by Mark Shelton

'A Practical Guide to Costs in Personal Injury Claims – 2nd Edition' by Matthew Hoe

'A Practical Guide to the General Data Protection Regulation (GDPR) – 2nd Edition' by Keith Markham

'Ellis on Credit Hire – Sixth Edition' by Aidan Ellis & Tim Kevan

'A Practical Guide to Working with Litigants in Person and McKenzie Friends in Family Cases' by Stuart Barlow

'Protecting Unregistered Brands: A Practical Guide to the Law of Passing Off' by Lorna Brazell

'A Practical Guide to Secondary Liability and Joint Enterprise Post-Jogee' by Joanne Cecil & James Mehigan

'A Practical Guide to the Pre-Action RTA Claims Protocol for Personal Injury Lawyers' by Antonia Ford

'A Practical Guide to Neighbour Disputes and the Law' by Alexander Walsh

'A Practical Guide to Forfeiture of Leases' by Mark Shelton

'A Practical Guide to Coercive Control for Legal Practitioners and Victims' by Rachel Horman

'A Practical Guide to Rights Over Airspace and Subsoil' by Daniel Gatty

'Tackling Disclosure in the Criminal Courts – A Practitioner's Guide' by Narita Bahra QC & Don Ramble

'A Practical Guide to the Law of Driverless Cars – Second Edition' by Alex Glassbrook, Emma Northey & Scarlett Milligan

'A Practical Guide to TOLATA Claims' by Greg Williams

'A Practical Guide to Elderly Law – 2nd Edition' by Justin Patten

'A Practical Guide to Responding to Housing Disrepair and Unfitness Claims' by Iain Wightwick

'A Practical Guide to the Construction and Rectification of Wills and Trust Instruments' by Edward Hewitt

'A Practical Guide to the Law of Bullying and Harassment in the Workplace' by Philip Hyland

'How to Be a Freelance Solicitor: A Practical Guide to the SRA-Regulated Freelance Solicitor Model' by Paul Bennett

'A Practical Guide to Prison Injury Claims' by Malcolm Johnson

'A Practical Guide to the Small Claims Track - 2nd Edition' by Dominic Bright

'A Practical Guide to Advising Clients at the Police Station'
by Colin Stephen McKeown-Beaumont

'A Practical Guide to Antisocial Behaviour Injunctions' by Iain Wightwick

'Practical Mediation: A Guide for Mediators, Advocates, Advisers, Lawyers, and
Students in Civil, Commercial, Business, Property, Workplace, and Employment
Cases' by Jonathan Dingle with John Sephton

'The Mini-Pupillage Workbook' by David Boyle

'A Practical Guide to Crofting Law' by Brian Inkster

'A Practical Guide to Spousal Maintenance' by Liz Cowell

'A Practical Guide to the Law of Domain Names and Cybersquatting'
by Andrew Clemson

'A Practical Guide to the Law of Gender Pay Gap Reporting' by Harini Iyengar

'A Practical Guide to the Rights of Grandparents in Children Proceedings'
by Stuart Barlow

'NHS Whistleblowing and the Law' by Joseph England

'Employment Law and the Gig Economy' by Nigel Mackay & Annie Powell

'A Practical Guide to Noise Induced Hearing Loss (NIHL) Claims'
by Andrew Mckie, Ian Skeate, Gareth McAloon

'An Introduction to Beauty Negligence Claims – A Practical Guide for the Personal
Injury Practitioner' by Greg Almond

'Intercompany Agreements for Transfer Pricing Compliance' by Paul Sutton

'Zen and the Art of Mediation' by Martin Plowman

'A Practical Guide to the SRA Principles, Individual and Law Firm Codes of
Conduct 2019 – What Every Law Firm Needs to Know' by Paul Bennett

'A Practical Guide to Adoption for Family Lawyers' by Graham Pegg

'A Practical Guide to Industrial Disease Claims' by Andrew Mckie & Ian Skeate

'A Practical Guide to Redundancy' by Philip Hyland

'A Practical Guide to Vicarious Liability' by Mariel Irvine

'A Practical Guide to Applications for Landlord's Consent and Variation of Leases'
by Mark Shelton

'A Practical Guide to Relief from Sanctions Post-Mitchell and Denton'
by Peter Causton

'A Practical Guide to Equity Release for Advisors' by Paul Sams
'A Practical Guide to Financial Services Claims' by Chris Hegarty
'The Law of Houses in Multiple Occupation: A Practical Guide to HMO Proceedings' by Julian Hunt
'Occupiers, Highways and Defective Premises Claims: A Practical Guide Post-Jackson – 2nd Edition' by Andrew Mckie
'A Practical Guide to Financial Ombudsman Service Claims' by Adam Temple & Robert Scrivenor
'A Practical Guide to Advising Schools on Employment Law' by Jonathan Holden
'A Practical Guide to Running Housing Disrepair and Cavity Wall Claims: 2nd Edition' by Andrew Mckie & Ian Skeate
'A Practical Guide to Holiday Sickness Claims – 2nd Edition' by Andrew Mckie & Ian Skeate
'Arguments and Tactics for Personal Injury and Clinical Negligence Claims' by Dorian Williams
'A Practical Guide to Drone Law' by Rufus Ballaster, Andrew Firman, Eleanor Clot
'A Practical Guide to Compliance for Personal Injury Firms Working With Claims Management Companies' by Paul Bennett
'RTA Allegations of Fraud in a Post-Jackson Era: The Handbook – 2nd Edition' by Andrew Mckie
'RTA Personal Injury Claims: A Practical Guide Post-Jackson' by Andrew Mckie
'On Experts: CPR35 for Lawyers and Experts' by David Boyle
'An Introduction to Personal Injury Law' by David Boyle

These books and more are available to order online direct from the publisher at www.lawbriefpublishing.com, where you can also read free sample chapters. For any queries, contact us on 0844 587 2383 or mail@lawbriefpublishing.com.

Our books are also usually in stock at www.amazon.co.uk with free next day delivery for Prime members, and at good legal bookshops such as Wildy & Sons.

We are regularly launching new books in our series of practical day-to-day practitioners' guides. Visit our website and join our free newsletter to be kept informed and to receive special offers, free chapters, etc.

You can also follow us on Twitter at www.twitter.com/lawbriefpub.